WITHDRAWN

## Think Like a Scientist

# Make a Research Plan

Caitie McAneney

**Britannica**
Educational Publishing

IN ASSOCIATION WITH

**ROSEN**
EDUCATIONAL SERVICES

Published in 2019 by Britannica Educational Publishing (a trademark of Encyclopædia Britannica, Inc.) in association with The Rosen Publishing Group, Inc.
29 East 21st Street, New York, NY 10010

Copyright © 2019 The Rosen Publishing Group, Inc. and Encyclopædia Britannica, Inc.
Encyclopædia Britannica, Britannica, and the Thistle logo are registered trademarks of Encyclopædia Britannica, Inc. All rights reserved.

Distributed exclusively by Rosen Publishing.
To see additional Britannica Educational Publishing titles, go to rosenpublishing.com.

First Edition

**Britannica Educational Publishing**
J.E. Luebering: Executive Director, Core Editorial
Mary Rose McCudden: Editor, Britannica Student Encyclopedia

**Rosen Publishing**
Amelie von Zumbusch: Editor
Nelson Sá: Art Director
Brian Garvey: Series Designer/Book Layout
Cindy Reiman: Photography Manager
Karen Huang: Photo Researcher

**Library of Congress Cataloging-in-Publication Data**

Names: McAneney, Caitie, author.
Title: Make a research plan / Caitie McAneney.
Description: New York : Britannica Educational Publishing, in Association with Rosen Educational Services, 2019. | Series: Think like a scientist | Audience: Grades 3–6. | Includes bibliographical references and index.
Identifiers: LCCN 2017044897| ISBN 9781538302262 (library bound)
| ISBN 9781538302279 (pbk.) | ISBN 9781538302286 (6 pack)
Subjects: LCSH: Science—Methodology—Juvenile literature. | Research—Juvenile literature.
Classification: LCC Q175.2 .M39275 2019 | DDC 507.2/1—dc23
LC record available at https://lccn.loc.gov/2017044897

Manufactured in the United States of America

**Photo credits:** Cover, p. 1 Rawpixel/iStock/Thinkstock; cover (top), back cover, interior pages background cetus/Shutterstock.com; p. 4 kali9/E+/Getty Images; p. 6 Samuel Borges Photography/Shutterstock.com; p. 7 © Encyclopædia Britannica, Inc; p. 9 © iStockphoto.com/Robert Ingelhart; p. 11 Jessica Wilson/Science Source; p. 12 VW Pics/Universal Images Group/Getty Images; pp. 13, 28 Hero Images/Getty Images; p. 14 James Gathany/Centers for Disease Control and Prevention (CDC); p. 16 © NOAA News October 2014; p. 17 © NOAA; p. 19 David Hay Jones/Science Source; p. 20 © AP Images; p. 21 Geoff Tompkinson/Science Source; p. 23 gosphotodesign/Shutterstock.com; p. 24 carballo/Shutterstock.com; p. 25 Susan Santa Maria/Shutterstock.com; p. 27 Jacek Chabraszewski/Shutterstock.com.

# CONTENTS

**CHAPTER 1**
Plan Like a Scientist! ......................... 4

**CHAPTER 2**
It All Starts with a Question ............... 8

**CHAPTER 3**
Real Scientists Research! ................... 14

**CHAPTER 4**
Let's Get Started! ............................ 22

Glossary ......................................... 30
For More Information ....................... 31
Index ............................................. 32

CHAPTER 1

# Plan Like a Scientist!

Have you ever performed an experiment? Do you remember the steps? To perform a scientific experiment, you need a good plan. Most start with a single question. For example, what happens when you mix baking soda and vinegar?

Some experiments involve mixing chemicals. Make sure a teacher is nearby!

Scientists are always questioning the natural world. They are naturally curious and wonder why things happen. Scientists follow a specific set of steps when they're developing a **theory** for why something is the way that it is. A research plan can lead them to a solution to their problem.

The process that scientists use to solve problems is called the scientific method. Scientists start by finding out as much as possible about a question or a problem. Then they make a hypothesis and test it through an experiment. Scientists use the information they learn from testing many hypotheses to develop scientific theories. This method helps scientists get accurate results that can be repeated.

## VOCABULARY

A **theory** is an explanation for why things work or how things happen.

The theory of gravity explains why an apple, or anything else, falls to the ground if you drop it.

You've probably heard "there's no such thing as a stupid question." That's true, but what makes a good scientific question? First, it must be testable. You wouldn't want to ask a question that can't be answered with experiments or measurements. It also has to have a real answer. For example, it is better to ask "At what temperature does water freeze?" than to ask "Why does my cat sleep so much?" The first question can be answered through observation and experimentation.

Scientific questions try to establish cause and effect. They look at how two situations are related. Scientific questions also try to see how different **variables** affect something. By asking a

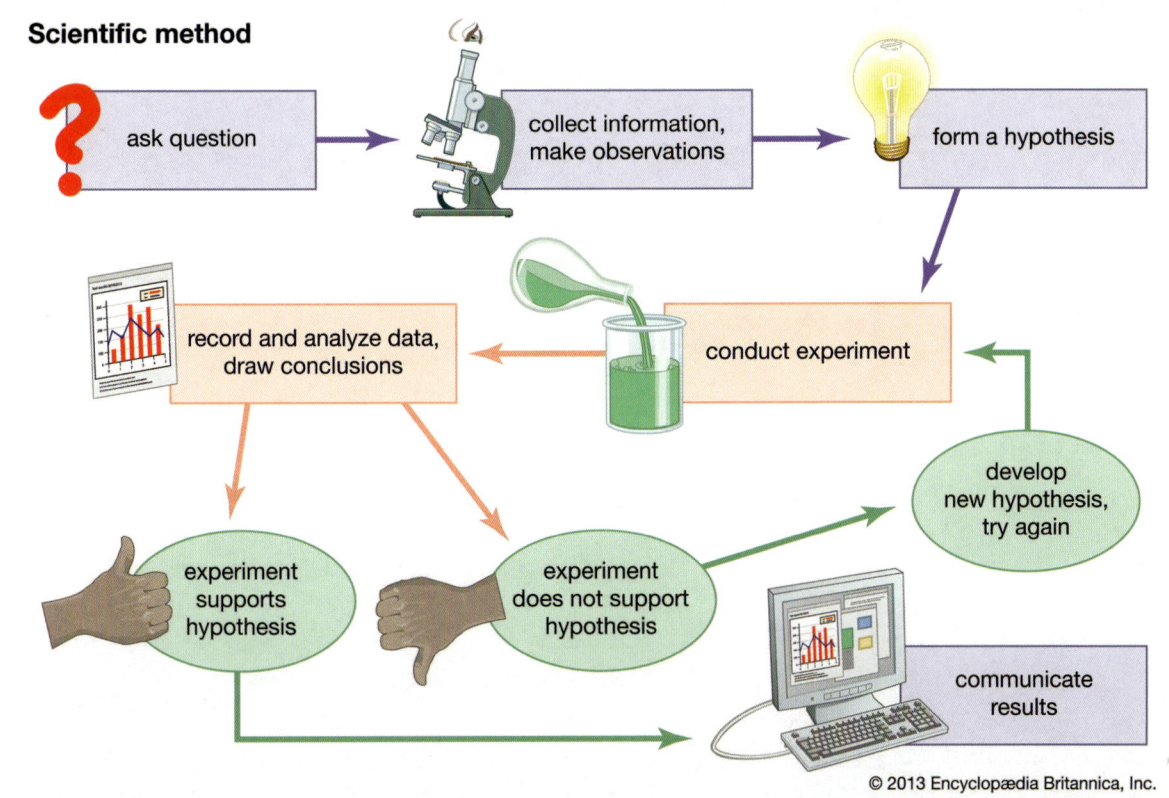

This chart shows the scientific method. You must follow each step to get accurate results!

## VOCABULARY

**Variables** are factors that can change within an experiment.

good question, a scientist can start constructing a research plan that follows the scientific method.

CHAPTER 2

# It All Starts with a Question

Everything we know in science started with a question. Some questions start with "why" or "how." Others start with "what happens." Once scientists have a question, they can start researching.

Scientists research all they can about a topic before they get started. Then, they can form a hypothesis. A hypothesis is an attempt to explain a problem. Scientists test a hypothesis with an experiment. If the experiment doesn't support the hypothesis, they have to think about the problem again and develop a new hypothesis.

Scientists always try to make the most specific hypothesis possible. A scientist might say, "I pre-

dict that sunlight and plant growth will be related." That's good, but it would be more specific if the scientist said instead, "I predict that the more sunlight I give my plant, the taller my plant will grow." That's called a directional hypothesis. It predicts the direction of the relationship between two things:

**Make your own hypothesis about this plant. Will sunlight make it grow?**

## THINK ABOUT IT

Think of something you will do later today, and come up with a directional hypothesis about it. For example, if I walk faster, I will get to the bus stop sooner. What are some others?

more sunlight leads to taller plants. A directional hypothesis is more specific. It's a better basis for an experiment.

Once scientists have a hypothesis, they come up with an experiment to prove the hypothesis right or wrong. Each step of the experiment must be well planned and then performed according to that plan. It must also be recorded in a detailed way.

Controlled experiments produce the most accurate results. A controlled experiment is performed under conditions the scientists can control. That means usually only one variable changes. The others stay constant.

Let's say the question scientists are testing is the effect of sunlight on plants.

## THINK ABOUT IT

What do you think would happen if you changed more than one variable at a time during an experiment? How would it affect data collection?

They would make everything in the experiment the same except for the one variable they are testing for—sunlight. Each plant would be the same species, all at the same stage of growth, in the same kind of soil, receiving the same amount of water. In this controlled experiment, scientists would give each plant a different level of sunlight. Then they would measure and write down how the different levels of sunlight affect each sample plant.

An experiment may test the effect of sunlight on plants. If the same type of plant is used throughout, the plant is a controlled variable.

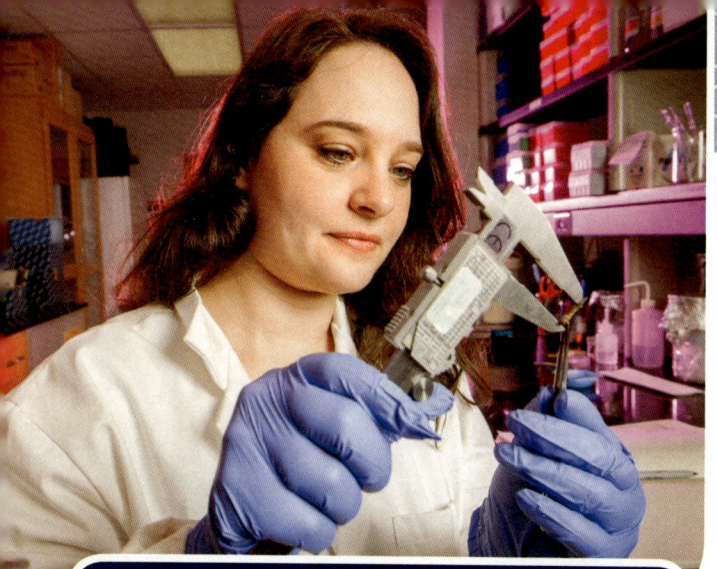

This scientist uses a measuring tool called a caliper. It measures the distance between the two sides of an object.

All scientists collect information, or data. Good scientists take measurements and observations before and after an experiment. That way, they can tell what changed. They also take measurements at specific intervals throughout the experiment. They might check at the same time every hour, every day, or every week. They are very specific in their measurements. They make sure to use the correct measuring tools. For example, thermometers measure temperature, and measuring tapes measure length.

## THINK ABOUT IT

What kinds of measuring tools could you use in an experiment?

After a scientist collects data, it's time to analyze it. Scientists look for patterns or trends in the data. They compare and contrast what happened under different variables.

If the hypothesis proves correct, a good scientist will do the experiment again and make sure the results can be repeated. If the results are not the same, the scientist would rework the hypothesis and start over. If the results can be repeated, then the scientist reports the findings in a scientific journal or meeting.

Scientists look at their data closely. It helps to make charts to better see patterns in data.

CHAPTER 3

# Real Scientists Research!

You might have performed an experiment in school. Maybe you were hoping for a good grade or a fun learning opportunity. But real scientists have to make research plans that will answer very important questions. Some research, such as medical research, might mean life and death for patients

This is a microbiologist in the medical field. She is testing blood samples in a lab.

suffering from a disease or injury. How do real scientists use research plans in their daily work?

Medical researchers look at how a certain medicine or other treatment affects patients. Cancer researchers might ask the question, "Are smoking habits and lung cancer related?" They might also ask, "What is the best medicine to treat lung cancer?" Answering these questions could save lives. The researchers must therefore plan their work very carefully. They make a hypothesis, and then they get to work making a plan to test their hypothesis. The plan would involve collecting data about patients. The data would have to include many factors, such as the age, health issues, and daily habits of the patients.

## THINK ABOUT IT

What are some other questions scientists in the medical field might ask?

Not all research jobs are in a lab! This oceanographer dives into the ocean to study it firsthand.

Oceanographers study the ocean. Some examine the quality of the water and the way the water moves. Others look at the structures of the sea-floors or the plants and animals that live in the ocean. What kinds of experiments would these scientists perform?

Oceanographers might ask the question, "How does an oil spill affect the population of sea turtles in a certain area?" They would have to be specific about the

**COMPARE & CONTRAST**

Consider the similarities and differences in research plans made by oceanographers and medical researchers.

species of turtle they want to study. If they were studying the effects of an oil spill after it already happened, they would need to know the population of sea turtles before the spill and after.

Oceanographers may also measure the temperature of the ocean as years go on. Their research plan would involve many measurements. They would have to attempt to keep the experiment as controlled as possible in such a wild environment.

Scientists who study climate are called climatologists. Climate is the weather in a place over a long period of time. Climatologists have many tools. They set up weather stations

**This climatologist is releasing a weather balloon from a weather station at the South Pole.**

on Earth to measure rainfall, temperature, and wind speed. They send weather balloons with special instruments up into the atmosphere. Weather satellites in space also report information to scientists on the ground. What kinds of experiments would these scientists perform?

Many climatologists study **global warming** and the causes for it. They may ask the question, "How does burning fossil fuels relate to global warming?"

To set up an experiment to answer this question, climatologists would have to collect and analyze a lot of data. They would look at the pattern of fossil fuel use over the course of time.

**VOCABULARY**

The average surface temperature on Earth is slowly increasing. This trend is known as **global warming**.

Some climatologists drill into deep ice using tools like this coring drill.

They would also look at how climates have changed over time.

Chemists are scientists who study the substances that make up matter. Matter is everything that takes up space. Chemists study the changes that take place when substances are combined. They can use that information to create new substances, such as plastics, fibers, medicines, and more.

Forensic chemists often have to test drugs in criminal investigations.

Chemists work in many different fields of science. A biochemist might develop new medicines. Another chemist might ask, "If we add this substance to plastic, would it make the plastic stronger?" They would look at the properties of the substance they were trying to add first. Then they would add the substance and test the new plastic to see if it is stronger than the original.

Some chemists develop medicines to help people get better. This chemist is testing a new medicine.

You can experiment like a chemist by mixing substances, such as oil and water, and observing what happens. Make observations as you experiment, just like a real chemist!

### THINK ABOUT IT

How can chemists use the information they learn about different substances to make new substances?

CHAPTER 4

# LET'S GET STARTED!

You don't need to be a professional scientist to make a research plan. You can ask questions and answer them through experimentation at home or at school. Let's get started!

Think of questions you want answered about the world. For example, which materials create a rainbow when light shines through them? Which **evaporates** faster, warm water or cold water? What happens when you mix sugar and water?

Be as specific as possible in your question. That will help you make the best research plan. For example, don't just ask, "What happens when I combine a solid and

**VOCABULARY**

When water **evaporates** it turns into a gas and moves into the air.

a liquid?" Instead ask, "What happens when I combine a certain amount of sugar with a certain amount of water?" Then, you know the exact materials you need. Remember, the best questions to ask are ones that you are really interested in!

Next, make a hypothesis based on your

**THINK ABOUT IT**

How can you use background knowledge and research to make an educated hypothesis?

What's your hypothesis about combining sugar and water? What do you already know about those two substances?

Write down your hypothesis. Make sure to keep detailed notes as you carry out your research plan.

question. Imagine you've chosen the question "What happens when you combine sugar and water?" You need to make a hypothesis about what you think will happen. This should be based on knowledge you already have about sugar and water. You can research before experimenting to make a more educated guess. Use book and online sources to learn as much as you can. In your research, you might come up with even more questions for experiments!

State your hypothesis using an "if, then" statement. For example, "I predict that if I combine sugar and water, then the sugar will dissolve in the water." It's okay if your hypothesis doesn't turn out to be correct. In fact, incorrect hypotheses can inspire new, interesting experiments.

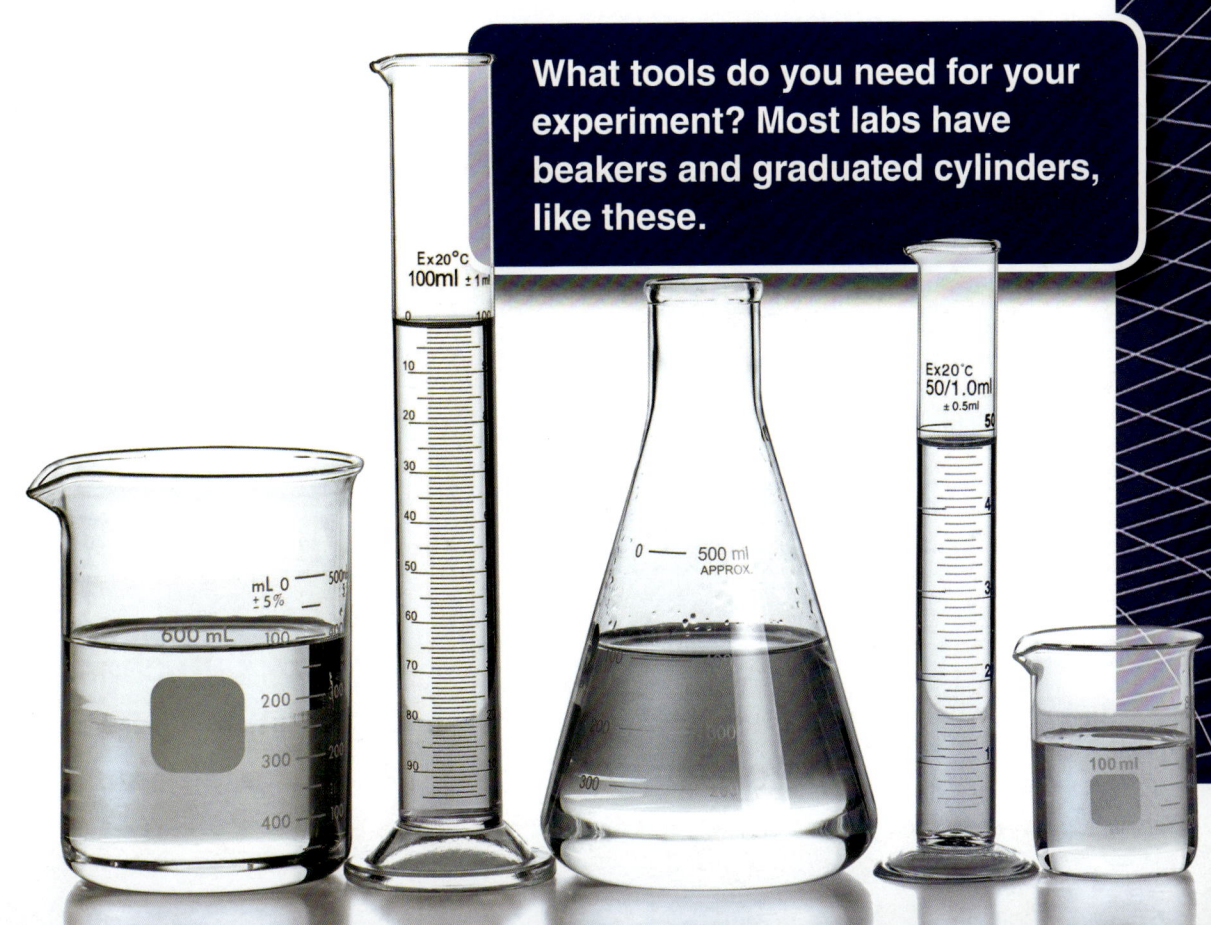

What tools do you need for your experiment? Most labs have beakers and graduated cylinders, like these.

It's easy to set up your own research plan once you have a hypothesis. First, think of the materials that you'll need. What is the variable? What is the subject of the experiment? In this case, you would collect a cup of water and a small amount of sugar.

Next, carry out your experiment. Ask yourself, how often should I take measurements or observe the experiment? In this case, you would drop sugar into water and observe it. Observe the water before sugar is added, right after, five minutes after, and one hour after. Your observations may include colors, textures, smells, and more.

Collect data in a notebook or a chart. If you have a lot of data, you can transfer it to a computer or tablet to make charts,

**THINK ABOUT IT**

How can charts and graphs help you use your data?

Be specific and careful when you collect data. Record everything you find!

graphs, and diagrams. These visuals will help you picture the data to better analyze it.

Once you have the results, analyze your data. Reconsider your hypothesis. Did it prove correct? If so, repeat the experiment to make sure it works again. If not, you can revise the hypothesis.

What if your research plan didn't give you an answer at all? Maybe you didn't ask a specific enough question. Maybe your research plan didn't test your question in a successful way. That's OK!

Teachers can show students how to plan and carry out experiments.

You can go back and make a new research plan.

When you do get results, share them with others. Make a presentation to your class describing your experiment. Present it at a science fair. You can show a flowchart of the steps you took in your research plan.

All experiments start with a single question. The plan you make to answer that question is your chance to use the scientific method.

**COMPARE & CONTRAST**

Describe the similarities and differences between how real scientists and students can report the results of their research plans.

# GLOSSARY

**accurate** Free from mistakes.
**analyze** To study or find out the nature and relationship of parts.
**cancer** A disease in which harmful masses spread in the body.
**develop** To create or produce something.
**diagram** A drawing, sketch, plan, or chart that makes something clearer or easier to understand.
**disease** Illness.
**flowchart** A diagram that shows the step-by-step progression through a process or system.
**fossil fuels** A fuel that is formed in the earth from plant or animal remains, such as coal, oil, or natural gas.
**hypothesis** Something not proved but assumed to be true for purposes of argument or further study or investigation.

**injury** Hurt, damage, or loss received.
**interval** A period of time between events or states.
**observation** An act of gathering information by noting facts or occurrences.
**patient** An individual awaiting or under medical care and treatment.
**perform** To do something requiring special skill.
**prediction** The act of guessing what will happen in the future.
**relate** To have a connection.
**research** To study something deeply.
**revise** To look over again in order to correct or improve.
**species** Things that are the same kind with the same name.

# FOR MORE INFORMATION

Ardley, Neil. *101 Great Science Experiments*. London, UK: DK Children, 2014.

Coleman, Miriam. *Women in Science*. New York, NY: PowerKids Press, 2015.

Franco, Michou. *I Can Be a Scientist*. New York, NY: Gareth Stevens Publishing, 2017.

Howell, Sara. *Chemists at Work*. New York, NY: Britannica Educational Publishing, 2018.

Polinsky, Paige V. *Super Simple Experiments with Mass: Fun and Innovative Science Projects*. Minneapolis, MN: Super Sandcastle, 2016.

Sohn, Emily. *Experiments in Earth Science and Weather with Toys and Everyday Stuff*. Mankato, MN: Capstone Press, 2015.

## WEBSITES

**Exploratorium**
https://www.exploratorium.edu
Twitter, Facebook, Instagram: @exploratorium

**Science Buddies**
https://www.sciencebuddies.org/science-fair-projects/science-fair/writing-a-science-fair-project-research-plan
Twitter, Facebook: @ScienceBuddies

**Science Journal for Kids**
http://www.sciencejournalforkids.org
Twitter: @SJforKids, Facebook: @sciencejournalforkids

# INDEX

analysis, 13, 18, 27

biochemists, 20

cause and effect, 6
charts, 26
chemists, 19–21
climatologists, 17–19
controlled experiments, 10, 11, 17

data collection, 10, 12, 13, 15, 18, 26
directional hypothesis, 9–10

evaporation, 22

flowchart, 29

global warming, 18
graphs, 26, 27

hypothesis, 5, 8–9, 10, 13, 15, 23–25, 26, 27

"if, then" statements, 25

measurements, 6, 11, 12, 17, 18, 26
measuring tools, 12
medical research, 14–15, 16
medicine, 20

observation, 6, 12, 21, 26
oceanographers, 16–17

presentations, 29

question, how to formulate one for research, 4, 6–7, 22–23

repeatable results, 5, 13
research plan, process for making one, 22–29

scientific method, 5, 29

variables, 6, 7, 10, 11, 13, 26

weather balloons, 18
weather satellites, 18
weather stations, 17